SONGS
of
CHILDHOOD

Under the Dock Leaves,
by Richard Doyle.

SONGS
of
CHILDHOOD

Walter de la Mare

Dover Publications, Inc.
New York

This Dover edition, first published in 1968, is an unabridged and unaltered republication of the work originally published by Longmans, Green, and Company in London in 1902, as *Songs of Childhood* by Walter Ramal.

Library of Congress Catalog Card Number: 68-28405

Manufactured in the United States of America
Dover Publications, Inc.
180 Varick Street
New York, N. Y. 10014

CONTENTS

'UNDER THE DOCK LEAVES' *Frontispiece*
    From a drawing by RICHARD DOYLE *in the possession of* C. J. LONGMAN, Esq.

	PAGE
THE GNOMIES	1
BLUEBELLS	3
LOVELOCKS,	4
O DEAR ME!	5
TARTARY	6
THE BUCKLE	8
THE HARE,	9
BUNCHES OF GRAPES	10
JOHN MOULDY	11
THE FLY	12
SONG	13
I SAW THREE WITCHES	14
THE SILVER PENNY	16

CONTENTS

	PAGE
THE NIGHT-SWANS	18
THE FAIRIES DANCING	20
REVERIE	22
THE THREE BEGGARS	24
THE DWARF	27
ALULVAN	30
THE PEDLAR	32
THE GREY WOLF	36
THE OGRE	37
DAME HICKORY	41
THE PILGRIM	43
THE GAGE	48
AS LUCY WENT A-WALKING	53
THE ENGLISHMAN	58
THE PHANTOM	62
THE MILLER AND HIS SON	68
DOWN-ADOWN-DERRY	71
THE SUPPER	75
THE ISLE OF LONE	78

CONTENTS

	PAGE
THE SLEEPING BEAUTY	83
THE HORN	84
CAPTAIN LEAN	85
THE PORTRAIT OF A WARRIOR	87
HAUNTED	88
THE RAVEN'S TOMB	90
THE CHRISTENING	91
THE MOTHER BIRD	93
THE CHILD IN THE STORY GOES TO BED	94
THE CHILD IN THE STORY AWAKES	96
THE LAMPLIGHTER	98
CECIL	100
I MET AT EVE	102
LULLABY	104
ENVOY	106

SONGS
of
CHILDHOOD

THE GNOMIES

As I lay awake in the white moonlight,
I heard a sweet singing in the wood—
  ' Out of bed,
  Sleepyhead,
  Put your white foot now,
  Here are we,
  'Neath the tree,
  Singing round the root now!'

I looked out of window in the white moonlight,
The trees were like snow in the wood—
  ' Come away
  Child and play,
  Light wi' the gnomies;
  In a mound,
  Green and round,
  That's where their home is!

THE GNOMIES

    ' Honey sweet,
    Curds to eat,
    Cream and frumènty,
    Shells and beads,
    Poppy seeds,
    You shall have plenty.'

But soon as I stooped in the dim moonlight
To put on my stocking and my shoe,
The sweet, sweet singing died sadly away,
And the light of the morning peep'd through:
Then instead of the gnomies there came a red robin
To sing of the buttercups and dew.

BLUEBELLS

WHERE the bluebells and the wind are,
Fairies in a ring I spied,
And I heard a little linnet
Singing near beside.

Where the primrose and the dew are,
Soon were sped the fairies all:
Only now the green turf freshens,
And the linnets call.

LOVELOCKS

I watched the Lady Caroline
Bind up her dark and beauteous hair;
Her face was rosy in the glass,
And 'twixt the coils her hands would pass,
    White in the candleshine.

Her bottles on the table lay,
Stoppered yet sweet of violet;
Her image in the mirror stooped
To view those locks as lightly looped
    As cherry-boughs in May.

The snowy night lay dim without,
I heard the Waits their sweet song sing;
The window smouldered keen with frost;
Yet still she twisted, sleeked and tossed
    Her beauteous hair about.

O DEAR ME!

HERE are crocuses, white, gold, grey!
  'O dear me!' says Marjorie May;
Flat as a platter the blackberry blows:
  'O dear me!' says Madeleine Rose;
The leaves are fallen, the swallows flown :
  'O dear me!' says Humphrey John;
Snow lies thick where all night it fell:
  'O dear me!' says Emmanuel.

TARTARY

If I were Lord of Tartary,
    Myself and me alone,
My bed should be of ivory,
    Of beaten gold my throne;
And in my court should peacocks flaunt,
And in my forests tigers haunt,
And in my pools great fishes slant
    Their fins athwart the sun.

If I were Lord of Tartary,
    Trumpeters every day
To all my meals should summon me,
    And in my courtyards bray;
And in the evenings lamps should shine,
Yellow as honey, red as wine,
While harp, and flute, and mandoline,
    Made music sweet and gay.

TARTARY

If I were Lord of Tartary,
    I'd wear a robe of beads,
White, and gold, and green they'd be—
    And small, and thick as seeds;
And ere should wane the morning-star,
I'd don my robe and scimitar,
And zebras seven should draw my car
    Through Tartary's dark glades.

Lord of the fruits of Tartary,
    Her rivers silver-pale!
Lord of the hills of Tartary,
    Glen, thicket, wood, and dale!
Her flashing stars, her scented breeze,
Her trembling lakes, like foamless seas,
Her bird-delighting citron-trees
    In every purple vale!

THE BUCKLE

I HAD a silver buckle,
I sewed it on my shoe,
And 'neath a sprig of mistletoe
I danced the evening through!

I had a bunch of cowslips,
I hid 'em in a grot,
In case the elves should come by night
And me remember not.

I had a yellow riband,
I tied it in my hair,
That, walking in the garden,
The birds might see it there.

I had a secret laughter,
I laughed it near the wall:
Only the ivy and the wind
May tell of it at all.

THE HARE

In the black furrow of a field
I saw an old witch-hare this night;
And she cocked her lissome ear,
And she eyed the moon so bright,
And she nibbled o' the green;
And I whispered 'Whsst! witch-hare,'
Away like a ghostie o'er the field
She fled, and left the moonlight there.

BUNCHES OF GRAPES

'Bunches of grapes,' says Timothy;
'Pomegranates pink,' says Elaine;
'A junket of cream and a cranberry tart
　For me,' says Jane.

'Love-in-a-mist,' says Timothy;
'Primroses pale,' says Elaine;
'A nosegay of pinks and mignonette
　For me,' says Jane.

'Chariots of gold,' says Timothy;
'Silvery wings,' says Elaine;
'A bumpity ride in a wagon of hay
　For me,' says Jane.

JOHN MOULDY

I SPIED John Mouldy in his cellar,
Deep down twenty steps of stone;
In the dusk he sat a-smiling,
  Smiling there alone.

He read no book, he snuffed no candle;
The rats ran in, the rats ran out;
And far and near, the drip of water
  Went whisp'ring about.

The dusk was still, with dew a-falling,
I saw the Dog-star bleak and grim,
I saw a slim brown rat of Norway
  Creep over him.

I spied John Mouldy in his cellar,
Deep down twenty steps of stone;
In the dusk he sat a-smiling,
  Smiling there alone.

THE FLY

How large unto the tiny fly
    Must little things appear !—
A rosebud like a feather bed,
    Its prickle like a spear;

A dewdrop like a looking-glass,
    A hair like golden wire ;
The smallest grain of mustard-seed
    As fierce as coals of fire;

A loaf of bread, a lofty hill;
    A wasp, a cruel leopard ;
And specks of salt as bright to see
    As lambkins to a shepherd.

SONG

O FOR a moon to light me home!
　O for a lanthorn green!
For those sweet stars the Pleiades,
That glitter in the twilight trees;
　O for a lovelorn taper! O
　For a lanthorn green!

O for a frock of tartan!
　O for clear, wild, grey eyes!
For fingers light as violets,
'Neath branches that the blackbird frets;
　O for a thistly meadow! O
　For clear, wild grey eyes!

O for a heart like almond boughs!
　O for sweet thoughts like rain!
O for first-love like fields of grey,
Shut April-buds at break of day!
　O for a sleep like music!
　For still dreams like rain!

I SAW THREE WITCHES

I saw three witches
That bowed down like barley,
And took to their brooms 'neath a louring sky,
And, mounting a storm-cloud,
Aloft on its margin,
Stood black in the silver as up they did fly.

I saw three witches
That mocked the poor sparrows
They carried in cages of wicker along,
Till a hawk from his eyrie
Swooped down like an arrow,
And smote on the cages, and ended their song.

I saw three witches
That sailed in a shallop,
All turning their heads with a truculent smile,

I SAW THREE WITCHES

Till a bank of green osiers
Concealed their grim faces,
Though I heard them lamenting for many a mile.

I saw three witches
Asleep in a valley,
Their heads in a row, like stones in a flood,
Till the moon, creeping upward,
Looked white through the valley,
And turned them to bushes in bright scarlet bud.

THE SILVER PENNY

'Sailorman, I'll give to you
   My bright silver penny,
If out to sea you'll sail me
   And my dear sister Jenny.'

'Get in, young sir, I'll sail ye
   And your dear sister Jenny,
But pay she shall her golden locks
   Instead of your penny.'

They sail away, they sail away,
   O fierce the winds blew!
The foam flew in clouds,
   And dark the night grew!

And all the wild sea-water
   Climbed steep into the boat;
Back to the shore again
   Sail they will not.

Drowned is the sailorman,
  Drowned is sweet Jenny,
And drowned in the deep sea
  A bright silver penny.

THE NIGHT-SWANS

'Tis silence on the enchanted lake,
And silence in the air serene,
Save for the beating of her heart,
The lovely-eyed Evangeline.

She sings across the waters clear
And dark with trees and stars between,
The notes her fairy godmother
Taught her, the child Evangeline.

As might the unrippled pool reply,
Faltering an answer far and sweet,
Three swans as white as mountain snow
Swim mantling to her feet.

And still upon the lake they stay,
Their eyes black stars in all their snow,
And softly, in the glassy pool,
Their feet beat darkly to and fro.

THE NIGHT-SWANS

She rides upon her little boat,
Her swans swim through the starry sheen,
Rowing her into Fairyland—
The lovely-eyed Evangeline.

'Tis silence on the enchanted lake,
And silence in the air serene;
Voices shall call in vain again
On earth the child Evangeline.

'Evangeline! Evangeline!'
Upstairs, downstairs, all in vain.
Her room is dim; her flowers faded;
She answers not again.

THE FAIRIES DANCING

I HEARD along the early hills,
Ere yet the lark was risen up,
Ere yet the dawn with firelight fills
The night-dew of the bramble-cup,—
I heard the fairies in a ring
Sing as they tripped a lilting round
Soft as the moon on wavering wing.
The starlight shook as if with sound,
As if with echoing, and the stars
Prankt their bright eyes with trembling gleams;
While red with war the gusty Mars
Rained upon earth his ruddy beams.
He shone alone, adown the West,
While I, behind a hawthorn-bush,
Watched on the fairies flaxen-tressed
The fires of the morning flush.
Till, as a mist, their beauty died,
Their singing shrill and fainter grew;

And daylight tremulous and wide
Flooded the moorland through and through;
Till Urdon's copper weathercock
Was reared in golden flame afar,
And dim from moonlit dreams awoke
The towers and groves of Arroar.

REVERIE

When slim Sophia mounts her horse
    And paces down the avenue,
It seems an inward melody
    She paces to.

Each narrow hoof is lifted high
    Beneath the dark enclust'ring pines,
A silver ray within his bit
    And bridle shines.

His eye burns deep, his tail is arched,
    And streams upon the shadowy air,
The daylight sleeks his jetty flanks,
    His mistress' hair.

Her habit flows in darkness down,
    Upon the stirrup rests her foot,
Her brow is lifted, as if earth
    She heeded not.

REVERIE

'Tis silent in the avenue,
   The sombre pines are mute of song,
The blue is dark, there moves no breeze
     The boughs among.

When slim Sophia mounts her horse
   And paces down the avenue,
It seems an inward melody
     She paces to.

THE THREE BEGGARS

'Twas autumn daybreak gold and wild,
　　While past St. Ann's grey tower they shuffled,
Three beggars spied a fairy-child
　　In crimson mantle muffled.

The daybreak lighted up her face
　　All pink, and sharp, and emerald-eyed;
She looked on them a little space,
　　And shrill as hautboy cried:—

'O three tall footsore men of rags
　　Which walking this gold morn I see,
What will ye give me from your bags
　　For fairy kisses three?'

The first, that was a reddish man,
　　Out of his bundle takes a crust:
'La, by the tombstones of St. Ann,
　　There's fee, if fee ye must!'

The second, that was a chesnut man,
   Out of his bundle draws a bone:
'La, by the belfry of St. Ann,
     And all my breakfast gone!'

The third, that was a yellow man,
   Out of his bundle picks a groat,
'La, by the Angel of St. Ann,
     And I must go without.'

That changeling, lean and icy-lipped,
   Touched crust, and bone, and groat, and lo!
Beneath her finger taper-tipped
     The magic all ran through.

Instead of crust a peacock pie,
   Instead of bone sweet venison,
Instead of groat a white lilie
     With seven blooms thereon.

And each fair cup was deep with wine:
   Such was the changeling's charity,
The sweet feast was enough for nine,
     But not too much for three.

O toothsome meat in jelly froze!
O tender haunch of elfin stag!
O rich the odour that arose!
O plump with scraps each bag!

There, in the daybreak gold and wild,
Each merry-hearted beggar man
Drank deep unto the fairy child,
And blessed the good St. Ann.

THE DWARF

'Now, Jinnie, my dear, to the dwarf be off,
    That lives in Barberry Wood,
And fetch me some honey, but be sure you don't
    laugh,—
  He hates little girls that are rude, are rude,
    He hates little girls that are rude.'

Jane tapped at the door of the house in the wood,
    And the dwarf looked over the wall,
He eyed her so queer, 'twas as much as she could
  To keep from laughing at all, at all,
    To keep from laughing at all.

His shoes down the passage came clod, clod, clod,
    And when he opened the door,
He croaked so harsh, 'twas as much as she could
  To keep from laughing the more, the more,
    To keep from laughing the more.

As there, with his bushy red beard, he stood,
    Pricked out to double its size,
He squinted so cross, 'twas as much as she could
    To keep the tears out of her eyes, her eyes,
       To keep the tears out of her eyes.

He slammed the door, and went clod, clod, clod,
    But while in the porch she bides,
He squealed so fierce, 'twas as much as she could
    To keep from cracking her sides, her sides,
       To keep from cracking her sides.

He threw a pumpkin over the wall,
    And melons and apples beside,
So thick in the air, that to see 'em all fall,
    She laughed, and laughed, till she cried, cried, cried,
       Jane laughed and laughed till she cried.

Down fell her teardrops a pit-apat-pat,
    And red as a rose she grew;—
'Kah! kah!' said the dwarf, 'is it crying you're at?
    It's the very worst thing you could do, do, do,
       It's the very worst thing you could do.'

He slipped like a monkey up into a tree,
    He shook her down cherries like rain;
'See now,' says he, cheeping, 'a blackbird I be,
    Laugh, laugh, little Jinnie, again-gain-gain,
    Laugh, laugh, little Jinnie, again.'

Ah me! what a strange, what a gladsome duet
    From a house i' the deeps of a wood!
Such shrill and such harsh voices never met yet
    A-laughing as loud as they could-could-could,
    A-laughing as loud as they could.

Come Jinnie, come dwarf, cocksparrow, and bee,
    There's a ring gaudy-green in the dell,
Sing, sing, ye sweet cherubs, that flit in the tree;
    La! who can draw tears from a well-well-well,
    Who ever drew tears from a well!

ALULVAN

THE sun is clear of bird and cloud,
The grass shines windless, grey, and still,
In dusky ruin the owl dreams on,
The cuckoo echoes on the hill;
    Yet soft along Alulvan's walks
      The ghost at noonday stalks.

His eyes in shadow of his hat
Stare on the ruins of his house;
His cloak, up-fasten'd with a brooch,
Of faded velvet grey as mouse,
    Brushes the roses as he goes:
      Yet wavers not one rose.

The wild birds in a cloud fly up
From their sweet feeding in the fruit;
The droning of the bees and flies
Rises gradual as a lute;
    Is it for fear the birds are flown,
      And shrills the insect-drone?

ALULVAN

Thick is the ivy o'er Alulvan,
And crisp with summer-heat its turf;
Far, far across its empty pastures
Alulvan's sands are white with surf:
   And he himself is grey as sea,
     Watching beneath an elder-tree.

All night the fretful, shrill Banshee
Lurks in the chambers' dark festoons,
Calling for ever, o'er garden and river,
Through magpie changing of the moons:
   'Alulvan, O, alas! Alulvan,
     The doom of lone Alulvan!'

THE PEDLAR

THERE came a Pedlar to an evening house;
Sweet Lettice, from her lattice looking down,
Wondered what man he was, so curious
His black hair dangled on his tattered gown:
Then lifts he up his face, with glittering eyes,—
'What will you buy, sweetheart?—Here's honey-
 comb,
And mottled pippins, and sweet mulberry pies,
Comfits and peaches, snowy cherry bloom,
To keep in water for to make night sweet:
All that you want, sweetheart,—come, taste and
 eat!'

Ev'n with his sugared words, returned to her
The clear remembrance of a gentle voice:—
'And O! my child, should ever a flatterer
Tap with his wares, and promise of all joys

And vain sweet pleasures that on earth may be;
Seal up your ears, sing some old happy song,
Confuse his magic who is all mockery:
His sweets are death.' Yet, still, how she doth long
But just to taste, then shut the lattice tight,
And hide her eyes from the delicious sight!

'What must I pay?' she whispered. 'Pay!' says he,
'Pedlar I am who through this wood do roam,
One lock of hair is gold enough for me,
For apple, peach, comfit, or honeycomb!'
But from her bough a drowsy squirrel cried,
'Trust him not, Lettice, trust, oh trust him not!'
And many another woodland tongue beside
Rose softly in the silence—'Trust him not!'
Then cried the Pedlar in a bitter voice,
'What, in the thicket, is this idle noise?'

A late, harsh blackbird smote him with her wings,
As through the glade, dark in the dim, she flew;
Yet still the Pedlar his old burden sings,—
'What, pretty sweetheart, shall I show to you?
Here's orange ribands, here's a string of pearls,
Here's silk of buttercup and pansy glove,

A pin of tortoiseshell for windy curls,
A box of silver, scented sweet with clove:
Come now,' he says, with dim and lifted face,
'I pass not often such a lonely place.'

'Pluck not a hair!' a hidden rabbit cried,
'With but one hair he'll steal thy heart away,
Then only sorrow shall thy lattice hide:
Go in! all honest pedlars come by day.'
There was dead silence in the drowsy wood;
'Here's syrup for to lull sweet maids to sleep;
And bells for dreams, and fairy wine and food
All day thy heart in happiness to keep';—
And now she takes the scissors on her thumb,—
'O, then, no more unto my lattice come!'

O sad the sound of weeping in the wood!
Now only night is where the Pedlar was;
And bleak as frost upon a too-sweet bud
His magic steals in darkness, O alas!
Why all the summer doth sweet Lettice pine?
And, ere the wheat is ripe, why lies her gold
Hid 'neath fresh new-pluckt sprigs of eglantine?
Why all the morning hath the cuckoo tolled,
Sad to and fro in green and secret ways,
With lonely bells the burden of his days?

THE PEDLAR

And, in the market-place, what man is this
Who wears a loop of gold upon his breast,
Stuck heartwise; and whose glassy flatteries
Take all the townsfolk ere they go to rest
Who come to buy and gossip? Doth his eye
Remember a face lovely in a wood?
O people! hasten, hasten, do not buy
His woful wares; the bird of grief doth brood
There where his heart should be; and far away
Dew lies on grave-flowers this selfsame day!

THE GREY WOLF

'A FAGOT, a fagot, go fetch for the fire, son!'
　'O, Mother, the wolf looks in at the door!'
'Cry Shoo! now, cry Shoo! thou fierce grey wolf fly, now;
　Haste thee away, he will fright thee no more.'

'I ran, O, I ran, but the grey wolf ran faster,
　O, Mother, I cry in the air at thy door,
Cry Shoo! now, cry Shoo! but his fangs were so cruel,
　Thy son (save his hatchet) thou'lt never see more.'

THE OGRE

'Tis moonlight on Trebarwith Vale,
　　And moonlight on an Ogre keen,
Who prowling hungry through the dale
　　A lone cottage hath seen.

Small with thin smoke ascending up
　　Three casements and a door:—
The Ogre eager is to sup,
　　And here seems dainty store.

Sweet as a larder to a mouse,
　　So to him staring down,
Seemed the sweet-windowed moonlit house,
　　With jasmine overgrown.

He snorted, as the billows snort
　　In darkness of the night,
Betwixt his lean locks tawny-swart,
　　He glowered on the sight.

THE OGRE

Into the garden sweet with peas
   He put his wooden shoe,
And bending back the apple trees
   Crept covetously through;

Then, stooping, with an impious eye
   Stared through the lattice small,
And spied two children which did lie
   Asleep, against the wall.

Into their dreams no shadow fell
   Of his disastrous thumb
Groping discreet, and gradual,
   Across the quiet room.

But scarce his nail had scraped the cot
   Wherein these children lay,
As if his malice were forgot,
   It suddenly did stay.

For faintly in the ingle-nook
   He heard a cradlesong,
That rose into his thoughts and woke
   Terror them among.

THE OGRE

For she who in the kitchen sat
   Darning by the fire,
Guileless of what he would be at,
   Sang sweet as wind or wire:—

'Lullay, thou little tiny child,
   By-by, lullay, lullie;
Jesu of glory, meek and mild,
   This night·remember ye!

'Fiend, witch, and goblin, foul and wild,
   He deems 'em smoke to be;
Lullay, thou little tiny child,
   By-by, lullay, lullie!'

The Ogre lifted up his eyes
   Into the moon's pale ray,
And gazed upon her leopard-wise,
   Cruel and clear as day;

He snarled in gluttony and fear:
   'The wind blows dismally,
Jesu in storm my lambs be near,
   By-by, lullay, lullie!'

THE OGRE

And like a ravenous beast which sees
   The hunter's icy eye,
So did this wretch in wrath confess
   Sweet Jesu's mastery.

He lightly drew his greedy thumb
   From out that casement pale,
And strode, enormous, swiftly home,
   Whinnying down the dale.

DAME HICKORY

'Dame Hickory, Dame Hickory,
Here's sticks for your fire,
Furze-twigs, and oak-twigs,
And beech-twigs, and briar!'
But when old Dame Hickory came for to see,
She found 'twas the voice of the false faerie.

'Dame Hickory, Dame Hickory,
Here's meat for your broth,
Goose-flesh, and hare's flesh,
And pig's trotters both!'
But when old Dame Hickory came for to see,
She found 'twas the voice of the false faerie.

'Dame Hickory, Dame Hickory,
Here's a wolf at your door,
His teeth grinning white,
And his tongue wagging sore!'
'Nay!' said Dame Hickory, 'ye false faerie!'
But a wolf 'twas indeed, and famished was he.

'Dame Hickory, Dame Hickory,
Here's buds for your tomb,
Bramble, and lavender,
And rosemary bloom!'
'Hush!' said Dame Hickory, 'ye false faerie,
Ye cry like a wolf, ye do, and trouble poor me.'

THE PILGRIM

'SHALL we carry now your bundle,
    You old grey man?

Over hill and over meadow,
Lighter than an owlet's shadow,
We will whirl it through the air,
Through blue regions shrill and bare;

Shall we carry now your bundle,
    You old grey man?'

The Pilgrim lifted up his eyes
And saw three fiends, in the skies,
Stooping o'er that lonely place
    Evil in form and face.

'O leave me, leave me, leave me,
    Ye three wild fiends!

Far it is my feet must wander,
And my city lieth yonder;
I must bear my bundle alone,
Help nor solace suffer none:

O leave me, leave me, leave me,
    Ye three wild fiends!'

The fiends stared down with greedy eye,
Fanning the chill air duskily,
'Twixt their hoods they stoop and cry:—

'Shall we smooth the path before you,
    You old grey man?

Sprinkle it green with gilded showers,
Strew it o'er with painted flowers?
Shall we blow sweet airs on it,
Lure the magpie there to flit?

Shall we smooth the path before you,
    You old grey man?'

THE PILGRIM

'O silence, silence, silence!
    Ye three wild fiends!

Over bog, and fen, and boulder,
I must bear it on my shoulder,
Beaten of wind, torn of briar,
Smitten of rain, parched of fire:

O silence, silence, silence!
    Ye three wild fiends!'

It seemed a smoke obscured the air,
Bright lightning quivered in the gloom,
And a faint voice of thunder spake
Far in the lone hill-hollows—'Come!'
Then half in fury, half in dread,
The fiends drew closer down and said:—

'Grey old man but sleep awhile;
    Sad old man!

Thorn, and dust, and ice, and heat;
Tarry now, sit down and eat;
Heat, and ice, and dust, and thorn;
Stricken, footsore, parched, forlorn,—
Juice of purple grape shall be
Youth and solace unto thee.

With sweet wire and reed we'll haunt you;
Songs of the valley shall enchant you;
Rest now, lest this night you die:
Sweet be now our lullaby:

'Grey old man, come sleep awhile,
    Stubborn old man!'

The pilgrim crouches terrified
At stooping hood, and glassy face,
Gloating, evil, side by side;
Terror and hate brood o'er the place;
He flings his withered hands on high
With a bitter, breaking cry:—

'Leave me, leave me, leave me, leave me,
    Ye three wild fiends:
If I lay me down in slumber,
    Then I lay me down in wrath;
If I stir not in sweet dreaming,
    Then I wither in my path;
If I hear sweet voices singing,
    'Tis a demon's lullaby,
And in "hideous storm and terror"
    Wake but to die!'

And even while he spake, the sun
From the sweet hills piercèd the gloom,
Kindling th' affrighted fiends upon.
Wild flapped their wings, as if in doom,
He heard a dismal hooting laughter:—

Nought but a little rain fell after,
And from the cloud whither they flew
A storm-sweet lark rose in the blue:
And his bundle seemed of flowers
    In his solitary hours.

THE GAGE

'Lady Jane, O Lady Jane!
Your hound hath broken bounds again,
  And chased my timorous deer, O;
    If him I see,
    That hour he'll dee;
  My brakes shall be his bier, O.'

'Lord Aërie, Lord Aërie,
My hound, I trow, is fleet and free,
  He's welcome to your deer, O;
    Shoot, shoot you may,
    He'll gang his way,
  Your threats we nothing fear, O.'

He's fetched him in, he's fetched him in,
Gone all his swiftness, all his din,
  White fang, and glowering eye, O:
    'Here is your beast,
    And now at least
  My herds in peace shall lie, O.'

THE GAGE

'"In peace!" my lord, O mark me well!
For what my jolly hound befell
  You shall sup twenty-fold, O!
    For every tooth
    Of his, i'sooth,
  A stag in pawn I hold, O.

'Huntsman and horn, huntsman and horn,
Shall scare your heaths and coverts lorn,
  Braying 'em shrill and clear, O;
    But lone and still
    Shall lift each hill,
  Each valley wan and sere, O.

'Ride up you may, ride down you may,
Lonely or trooped, by night or day,
  My hound shall haunt you ever:
    Bird, beast, and game
    Shall dread the same,
  The wild fish of your river.'

Her cheek is like the angry rose,
Her eye with wrath and pity flows:
  He gazes fierce and round, O,—
    'Dear Lord!' he says,
    'What loveliness
  To waste upon a hound, O.

THE GAGE

'I'd give my stags, my hills and dales,
My stormcocks and my nightingales
   To have undone this deed, O;
     For deep beneath
     My heart is death
   Which for her love doth bleed, O.'

Wanders he up, wanders he down,
On foot, a-horse, by night and noon:
   His lands are bleak and drear, O;
     Forsook his dales
     Of nightingales,
   Forsook his moors of deer, O.

Forsook his heart, ah me! of mirth;
There's nothing lightsome left on earth:
   Only one scene is fain, O,
     Where far remote
     The moonbeams gloat,
   And sleeps the lovely Jane, O.

Until an eve when lone he went,
Gnawing his beard in dreariment,
   Lo! from a thicket hidden,
     Lovely as flower
     In April hour,
   Steps forth a form unbidden.

THE GAGE

'Get ye now down, Lord Aërie,
I 'm troubled so I 'm like to dee,'
  She cries, 'twixt joy and grief, O ;
    ' The hound is dead,
    When all is said,
  But love is past belief, O.

'Nights, nights I 've lain your lands to see,
Forlorn and still—and all for me,
  All for a foolish curse, O ;
    Now here am I
    Come out to die,
  To live unlov'd is worse, O !'

In faith, this lord, in that lone dale,
Hears now a sweeter nightingale,
  And lairs a tend'rer deer, O ;
    His sorrow goes
    Like mountain snows
  In waters sweet and clear, O !

Let the hound bay in Shadowland,
Tuning his ear to understand
  What voice hath tamed this Aërie ;
    Chafe, chafe he may
    The stag all day,
  And never thirst nor weary.

Now here he smells, now there he smells,
Winding his voice along the dells,
   Till grey flows up the morn, O ;
     Then hies again
     To Lady Jane,
   No longer now forlorn, O.

Ay, as it were a bud, did break
To loveliness for Aërie's sake,
   So she in beauty moving
     Rides at his hand
     Across his land,
   Beloved as well as loving.

AS LUCY WENT A-WALKING

As Lucy went a-walking one wintry morning fine,
There sate three crows upon a bough, and three times three is nine:
Then 'O!' said Lucy, in the snow, 'it's very plain to see
A witch has been a-walking in the fields in front of me.'

Then stept she light and heedfully across the frozen snow,
And plucked a bunch of elder-twigs that near a pool did grow:
And, by and by, she comes to seven shadows in one place
All stretched by seven poplar-trees against the sun's bright face.

She looks to left, she looks to right, and in the
 midst she sees
A little well of water clear and frozen 'neath the
 trees;
Then down beside its margent in the crusty
 snow she kneels,
And hears a magic belfry a-ringing with sweet
 bells.

But when the belfry ceased to sound yet nothing
 could she see,
Save only frozen water in the shadow of the tree.
But presently she lifted up her eyes along the
 snow,
And sees a witch in brindled shawl a-frisking to
 and fro.

Her shoes were buckled scarlet that capered to
 and fro,
And all her rusty locks were wreathed with
 twisted mistletoe;
But never a dint, or mark, or print, in the white-
 ness for to see,
Though danced she high, though danced she fast,
 though danced she lissomely.

It seemed 'twas diamonds in the air, or little
 flakes of frost;
It seemed 'twas golden smoke around, or sun-
 beams lightly tost;
It seemed an elfin music like to reeds and
 warblers rose:
'Nay!' Lucy said, 'it is the wind that through
 the branches flows.'

And as she peeps, and as she peeps, 'tis no
 more one, but three,
And eye of bat, and downy wing of owl within
 the tree,
And the bells of that sweet belfry a-pealing as
 before,
And now it is not three she sees, and now it is
 not four.

'O! who are ye,' sweet Lucy cries, 'that in a
 dreadful ring,
All muffled up in brindled shawls, do caper,
 frisk, and spring?'
'A witch and witches, one and nine,' they
 straight to her reply,
And looked upon her narrowly, with green and
 needle eye.

Then Lucy sees in clouds of gold sweet cherry-trees upgrow,
And bushes of red roses that bloomed above the snow;
She smells all faint the almond-boughs that blow so wild and fair,
And doves with milky eyes ascend fluttering in the air.

Clear flow'rs she sees, like tulip buds, go floating by like birds,
With wavering tips that warbled sweetly strange enchanted words;
And as with ropes of amethyst the boughs with lamps were hung,
And clusters of green emeralds like fruit upon them clung.

'O witches nine, ye dreadful nine, O witches seven and three!
Whence come these wondrous things that I this Christmas morning see?'
But straight, as in a clap, when she of Christmas says the word,
Here is the snow, and there the sun, but never bloom nor bird;

Nor warbling flame, nor gloaming-rope of amethyst there shows,
Nor bunches of green emeralds, nor belfry, well, and rose,
Nor cloud of gold, nor cherry-tree, nor witch in brindled shawl,
But like a dream which vanishes, so vanished were they all.

When Lucy sees, and only sees, three crows upon a bough,
And earthly twigs, and bushes hidden white in driven snow,
Then 'O!' said Lucy, 'three times three is nine—I plainly see
Some witch has been a-walking in the fields in front of me.'

THE ENGLISHMAN

I MET a sailor in the woods,
   A silver ring wore he,
His hair hung black, his eyes shone blue,
   And thus he said to me:—

'What country, say, of this round earth,
   What shore of what salt sea,
Be this, my son, I wander in,
   And looks so strange to me?'

Says I, 'O foreign sailorman,
   In England now you be,
This is her wood, and this her sky,
   And that her roaring sea.'

He lifts his voice yet louder,
   'What smell be this,' says he,
'My nose on the sharp morning air
   Snuffs up so greedily?'

THE ENGLISHMAN

Says I, 'It is wild roses
  Do smell so winsomely,
And winy briar too,' says I,
  'That in these thickets be.'

'And oh!' says he, 'what leetle bird
  Is singing in yon high tree,
So every shrill and long-drawn note
  Like bubbles breaks in me?'

Says I, 'It is the mavis
  That perches in the tree,
And sings so shrill, and sings so sweet,
  When dawn comes up the sea.'

At which he fell a-musing,
  And fixed his eye on me,
As one alone 'twixt light and dark
  A spirit thinks to see

'England!' he whispers soft and harsh,
  'England!' repeated he,
'And briar, and rose, and mavis,
  A-singing in yon high tree.

'Ye speak me true, my leetle son,
   So—so, it came to me,
A-drifting landwards on a spar,
   And grey dawn on the sea.

'Ay, ay, I could not be mistook;
   I knew them leafy trees,
I knew that land so witcherie sweet,
   And that old noise of seas.

'Though here I've sailed a score of years,
   And heard 'em, dream or wake,
Lap small and hollow 'gainst my cheek,
   On sand and coral break;

'"Yet now," my leetle son, says I,
   A-drifting on the wave,
"That land I see so safe and green
   Is England, I believe.

'"And that there wood is English wood,
   And this here cruel sea,
The selfsame old blue ocean
   Years gone remembers me,

' " A-sitting with my bread and butter
   Down ahind yon chitterin' mill;
And this same Marinere "—(that's me),
   " Is that same leetle Will!—

' " That very same wee leetle Will
   Eating his bread and butter there,
A-looking on the broad blue sea
   Betwixt his yaller hair!"

' And here be I, my son, throwed up
   Like corpses from the sea,
Ships, stars, winds, tempests, pirates past,
   Yet leetle Will I be!'

He said no more, that sailorman,
   But in a reverie
Stared like the figure of a ship
   With painted eyes to sea.

THE PHANTOM

' UPSTAIRS in the large closet, child,
    This side the blue-room door,
Is an old Bible, bound in leather,
    Standing upon the floor;

' Go with this taper, bring it me;
    Carry it on your arm;
It is the book on many a sea
    Hath stilled the waves' alarm.'

Late the hour, dark the night,
    The house is solitary,
Feeble is a taper's light
    To light poor Ann to see.

Her eyes are yet with visions bright
    Of sylph and river, flower and fay,
Now through a narrow corridor
    She takes her lonely way.

THE PHANTOM

Vast shadows on the heedless walls
   Gigantic loom, stoop low:
Each little hasty footfall calls
   Hollowly to and fro.

In the dim solitude her heart
   Remembers tearlessly
White winters when her mother was
   Her loving company.

Now in the dark clear glass she sees
   A taper mocking hers,—
A phantom face of light blue eyes,
   Reflecting phantom fears.

Around her loom the vacant rooms,
   Wind the upward stairs,
She climbs on into a loneliness
   Only her taper shares.

Her grandmother is deaf with age;
   A garden of moonless trees
Would answer not though she should cry
   In anguish on her knees.

So that she scarcely heeds—so fast
    Her pent-up heart doth beat—
When, faint along the corridor,
    Falleth the sound of feet :—

Sounds lighter than silk slippers make
    Upon a ballroom floor, when sweet
Violin and 'cello wake
    Music for twirling feet.

O! in an old unfriendly house,
    What shapes may not conceal
Their faces in the open day,
    At night abroad to steal?

Even her taper seems with fear
    To languish small and blue;
Far in the woods the winter wind
    Runs whistling through.

A dreadful cold plucks at each hair,
    Her mouth is stretched to cry,
But sudden, with a gush of joy,
    It narrows to a sigh.

It is a wilding child which comes
  Swift through the corridor,
Singing an old forgotten song,
  This ancient burden bore:—

'Thorn, thorn, I wis,
And roses twain,
  A red rose and a white,
Stoop in the blossom, bee, and kiss
  A lonely child good-night.

'Swim fish, sing bird,
And sigh again,
  I that am lost am lone,
Bee in the blossom never stirred
  Locks hid beneath a stone!'—

Her eye was of the azure fire
  That hovers in wintry flame;
Her raiment wild and yellow as furze
  That spouteth out the same;

And in her hand she bore no flower,
  But on her head a wreath
Of faded flag-flowers that did yet
  Smell sweetly after death.

Clear was the light of loveliness
    That lit her face like rain;
And sad the mouth that uttered
    Her immemorial strain.

.   .   .   .   .

Gloomy with night the corridor
    Is now that she is gone,
Albeit this solitary child
    No longer seems alone.

Fast though her taper dwindles down,
    Heavy and thick the tome,
A beauty beyond fear to dim
    Haunts now her alien home.

Ghosts in the world malignant, grim,
    Vex many a wood, and glen,
And house, and pool,—the unquiet ghosts
    Of dead and restless men.

But in her grannie's house this spirit—
    A child as lone as she—
Pining for love not found on earth,
    Ann dreams again to see.

Seated upon her tapestry-stool,
  Her fairy-book laid by,
She gazes in the fire, knowing
  She hath sweet company.

THE MILLER AND HIS SON

A TWANGLING harp for Mary,
 A silvery flute for John,
And now we'll play the livelong day,
 'The Miller and his Son.'

'The Miller went a-walking
 All in the forest high,
He sees three doves a-flitting
 Against the dark blue sky:

'Says he, "My son, now follow
 These doves so white and free,
That cry above the forest,
 And surely cry to thee."

'"I go, my dearest Father,
 But O! I sadly fear,
These doves so white will lead me far,
 But never bring me near."

THE MILLER AND HIS SON

'He kisses the Miller,
   He cries, "Awhoop to ye!"
And straightway through the forest
   Follows the wood-doves three.

'There came a sound of weeping
   To the Miller in his Mill;
Red roses in a thicket
   Bloomed over near his wheel;

'Three stars shone wild and brightly
   Above the forest dim:
But never his dearest son
   Returns again to him.

'The cuckoo shall call "Cuckoo!"
   In vain along the vale,
The linnet, and the blackbird,
   The mournful nightingale;

'The Miller hears and sees not,
   A-thinking of his son;
His toppling wheel is silent;
   His grinding done.

'"Ye doves so white," he weepeth,
  "Ye roses on the tree,
Ye stars that shine so brightly,
  Ye shine in vain for me!"

'I bade him follow, follow,
  He said, "O Father dear,
These doves so white will lead me far
  But never bring me near!"'

A twangling harp for Mary,
  A silvery flute for John,
And now we'll play the livelong day,
  'The Miller and his Son.'

DOWN-ADOWN-DERRY

Down-adown-derry,
Sweet Annie Maroon,
Gathering daisies
In the meadows of Doone,
Sees a white fairy
Skip buxom and free
Where the waters go brawling
In rills to the sea;
    Singing down-adown-derry.

Down-adown-derry,
Sweet Annie Maroon
Through the green grasses
Runs fleetly and soon,
And lo! on a lily
She sees one recline
Whose eyes in her wee face
Like the water-sparks shine;
    Singing down-adown-derry.

Down-adown-derry,
And shrill was her tune :—
'Come to my water-house,
Annie Maroon,
Come in your pink gown,
Your curls on your head,
To wear the white samite
And rubies instead';
    Singing down-adown-derry.

'Down-adown-derry,
Lean fish of the sea,
Bring lanthorns for feasting
The gay Fäerie;
And it's dancing on sand 'tis
That's smoother than wool;—
Foam-fruit and wild honey
To pleasure you full';
    Singing down-adown-derry.

Down-adown-derry,
Sweet Annie Maroon
Looked large on the fairy
Curled wan as the moon;

And all the grey ripples
To the Mill racing by,
With harps and with timbrels
Did ringing reply;
    Singing down-adown-derry.

'Down-adown-derry,'
Sang the Fairy of Doone,
Piercing the heart of
Sweet Annie Maroon;
And lo! when like roses
The clouds of the sun
Faded at dusk, gone
Was Annie Maroon;
    Singing down-adown-derry.

Down-adown-derry,
The daisies are few;
Frost twinkles powd'ry
In haunts of the dew;
Only the robin
Perched on a white thorn,
Can comfort the heart of
A father forlorn;
    Singing down-adown-derry.

Down-adown-derry,
There's snow in the air;
Ice where the lily
Bloomed waxen and fair;
He may call o'er the water,
Cry—cry through the Mill,
But Annie Maroon, alas!
Answer ne'er will;
    Singing down-adown-derry.

THE SUPPER

A WOLF he pricks with eyes of fire
Across the night's o'ercrusted snows,
    Seeking his prey,
    He pads his way
Where Jane benighted goes,
  Where Jane benighted goes.

He curdles the bleak air with ire,
Ruffling his hoary raiment through,
    And lo ! he sees
    Beneath the trees
Where Jane's light footsteps go,
  Where Jane's light footsteps go.

No hound peals thus in wicked joy,
He snaps his muzzle in the snows,
    His five-clawed feet
    Do scamper fleet
Where Jane's bright lanthorn shows,
  Where Jane's bright lanthorn shows.

THE SUPPER

Now his greed's green doth gaze unseen
On a pure face of wilding rose,
    Her amber eyes
    In fear's surprise
Watch largely as she goes,
    Watch largely as she goes.

Salt wells his hunger in his jaws,
His lust it revels to and fro,
    Yet small beneath
    A soft voice saith,
' Jane shall in safety go,
    Jane shall in safety go.'

He lurched as if a fiery lash
Had scourged his hide, and through and through,
    His furious eyes
    O'erscanned the skies,
But nearer dared not go,
    But nearer dared not go.

He reared like wild Bucephalus,
His fangs like spears in him uprose,
    Ev'n to the town
    Jane's flitting gown
He grins on as she goes,
    He grins on as she goes.

THE SUPPER

In fierce lament he howls amain,
He scampers, marvelling in his throes
    What brought him there
    To sup on air,
While Jane unarmèd goes,
  While Jane unarmèd goes.

THE ISLE OF LONE

Three dwarfs there were which lived on an isle,
    And the name of the isle was Lone,
And the names of the dwarfs were Alliolyle,
    Lallerie, Muziomone.

Alliolyle was green of een,
    Lallerie light of locks,
Muziomone was mild of mien,
    As ewes in April flocks.

Their house was small and sweet of the sea,
    And pale as the Malmsey wine;
Their bowls were three, and their beds were three,
    And their nightcaps white were nine.

THE ISLE OF LONE

Their beds were of the holly-wood,
  Their combs of the tortoiseshell,
Their mirrors clear as wintry flood,
  Frozen dark and snell.

So each would lie on his plumpy pillow,
  The moon for company,
And hear the parrot scream to the billow,
  And the billow roar reply.—

Sulphur parrots, and parrots red,
  Scarlet, and flame, and green;
And five-foot apes that jargonèd
  In feathery-tufted treen.

And oh, or ever the dawning shed
  On dreams a narrow flame,
Three gaping dwarfs gat out of bed
  And gazed upon the same.

At dawn they fished, at noon they snared
  Young foxes in the dells,
At even on dew-berries they fared,
  And blew in their twisted shells.

Dark was the sea they gambolled in,
    And thick with silver fish,
Dark as green glass blown clear and thin
    To be a monarch's dish.

They sate to sup in a jasmine bower,
    Lit pale with flies of fire,
Their bowls the hue of the iris-flower,
    And lemon their attire.

Sweet wine in little cups they sipped,
    And golden honeycomb
Into their bowls of cream they dipped,
    Whipt light and white as foam.

Alliolyle, where the salt sea flows,
    Taught three old apes to sing,
And there to the moon, like a full-blown rose,
    They capered in a ring.

But down to the shore skipped Lallerie,
    His parrot on his thumb,
And the twain they scritched in mockery,
    While the dancers go and come.

So, alas! in the evening, rosy and still,
  Light-haired Lallerie
Bitterly quarrelled with Alliolyle
  By the yellow-sanded sea.

The rising moon swam sweet and large
  Before their furious eyes,
And they rolled and rolled to the coral marge
  Where the surf for ever cries.

Too late, too late, comes Muziomone:
  Clear in the clear green sea
Alliolyle lies not alone,
  But clasped with Lallerie.

He blows on his shell plaintive notes;
  Ape, parraquito, bee
Flock where a shoe on the salt wave floats,—
  The shoe of Lallerie.

He fetches nightcaps, one and nine,
  Grey apes he dowers three,
His house as fair as the Malmsey wine
  Seems sad as cypress-tree.

Three bowls he brims with honeycomb
    To feast the bumble bees,
Saying, 'O bees, be this your home,
    For grief is on the seas!'

He sate him lone in a coral grot,
    At the flowing of the tide;
When ebbed the billow, there was not,
    Save coral, aught beside.

So hairy apes in three white beds,
    And nightcaps, one and nine,
On moonlit pillows lay three heads
    Bemused with dwarfish wine.

A tomb of coral, the dirge of bee,
    The grey apes' guttural groan
For Alliolyle, for Lallerie,
    For thee, O Muziomone!

THE SLEEPING BEAUTY

THE scent of bramble sweets the air,
  Amid her folded sheets she lies,
The gold of evening in her hair,
  The blue of morn shut in her eyes.

How many a changing moon hath lit
  The unchanging roses of her face!
Her mirror ever broods on it
  In silver stillness of the days.

Oft flits the moth on filmy wings
  Into his solitary lair;
Shrill evensong the cricket sings
  From some still shadow in her hair.

In heat, in snow, in wind, in flood,
  She sleeps in lovely loneliness,
Half folded like an April bud
  On winter-haunted trees.

THE HORN

Hark! is that a horn I hear,
  In cloudland winding sweet—
And bell-like clash of bridle-rein,
  And silver-shod light feet?

Is it the elfin laughter of
  Fairies riding faint and high,
'Neath the branches of the moon,
  Straying through the starry sky?

Is it in the globèd dew
  Such sweet melodies may fall?
Wood and valley—all are still,
  Hushed the shepherd's call.

Hark! is that a horn I hear
  In cloudland winding sweet?
Or gloomy goblins marching out
  Their captain Puck to greet?

CAPTAIN LEAN

OUT of the East a hurricane
   Swept down on Captain Lean—
That mariner and gentleman
   Will ne'er again be seen.

He sailed his ship against the foes
   Of his own country dear,
But now in the trough of the billows
   An aimless course doth steer.

Powder was violets to his nostril,
   Sweet the din of the fighting-line,
Now he is flotsam on the seas,
   And his bones are bleached with brine.

The stars move up along the sky,
   The moon she shines so bright,
And in that solitude the foam
   Sparkles unearthly white.

CAPTAIN LEAN

This is the tomb of Captain Lean,
    Would a straiter please his soul?
I trow he sleeps in peace,
    Howsoever the billows roll!

THE PORTRAIT OF A WARRIOR

His brow is seamed with line and scar ;
  His cheek is red and dark as wine ;
The fires as of a Northern star
  Beneath his cap of sable shine.

His right hand, bared of leathern glove,
  Hangs open like an iron gin,
You stoop to see his pulses move,
  To hear the blood sweep out and in.

He looks some king, so solitary
  In earnest thought he seems to stand,
As if across a lonely sea
  He gazed impatient of the land.

Out of the noisy centuries
  The foolish and the fearful fade ;
Yet burn unquenched these warrior eyes,
  Time hath not dimmed nor death dismayed.

HAUNTED

From out the wood I watched them shine,—
    The windows of the haunted house,
Now ruddy as enchanted wine,
    Now dim as flittermouse.

There went a thin voice piping airs
    Along the grey and crooked walks,—
A garden of thistledown and tares,
    Bright leaves, and giant stalks.

The twilight rain shone at its gates,
    Where long-leaved grass in shadow grew;
And black in silence to her mates
    A voiceless raven flew.

Lichen and moss the lone stones greened,
    Green paths led lightly to its door,
Keen from her lair the spider leaned,
    And dusk to darkness wore.

Amidst the sedge a whisper ran,
  The West shut down a heavy eye,
And like last tapers, few and wan,
  The watch-stars kindled in the sky.

THE RAVEN'S TOMB

'Build me my tomb,' the Raven said,
'Within the dark yew-tree,
So in the Autumn yewberries
Sad lamps may burn for me.
Summon the haunted beetle,
From twilight bud and bloom,
To drone a gloomy dirge for me
At dusk above my tomb.
Beseech ye too the glowworm
To bear her cloudy flame,
Where the small, flickering bats resort,
Whistling in tears my name.
Let the round dew a whisper make,
Welling on twig and thorn;
And only the grey cock at night
Call through his silver horn.
And you, dear sisters, don your black
For ever and a day,
To show how sweet a raven
In his tomb is laid away.'

THE CHRISTENING

The bells chime clear,
Soon will the sun behind the hills sink down;
Come, little Ann, your baby brother dear
Lies in his christening-gown.

His godparents
Are all across the fields stepped on before,
And wait beneath the crumbling monuments,
This side the old church door.

Your mammie dear
Leans frail and lovely on your daddie's arm;
Watching her chick, 'twixt happiness and fear,
Lest he should come to harm.

All to be blest
Full soon in the clear heavenly water, he
Sleeps on unwitting of't, his little breast
Heaving so tenderly.

THE CHRISTENING

I carried you,
My little Ann, long since on this same quest,
And from the painted windows a pale hue
Lit golden on your breast;

And then you woke,
Chill as the holy water trickled down,
And, weeping, cast the window a strange look,
Half smile, half infant frown.

I scarce could hear
The larks a-singing in the green meadows,
'Twas summertide, and budding far and near
The hedges thick with rose.

And now you're grown
A little girl, and this same helpless mite
Is come like such another bud half-blown,
Out of the wintry night.

Time flies, time flies!
And yet, bless me! 'tis little changed am I;
May Jesu keep from tears those infant eyes,.
Be love their lullaby!

THE MOTHER BIRD

THROUGH the green twilight of a hedge
I peered, with cheek on the cool leaves pressed,
And spied a bird upon a nest:
Two eyes she had beseeching me
Meekly and brave, and her brown breast
Throbb'd hot and quick above her heart;
And then she oped her dagger bill,—
'Twas not a chirp, as sparrows pipe
At break of day; 'twas not a trill,
As falters through the quiet even;
But one sharp solitary note,
One desperate, fierce, and vivid cry
Of valiant tears, and hopeless joy,
One passionate note of victory:
Off, like a fool afraid, I sneaked,
Smiling the smile the fool smiles best,
At the mother bird in the secret hedge
Patient upon her lonely nest.

THE CHILD IN THE STORY
GOES TO BED

I PRYTHEE, Nurse, come smooth my hair,
    And prythee, Nurse, unloose my shoe,
And trimly turn my silken sheet
    Upon my quilt of gentle blue.

My pillow sweet of lavender
    Smooth with an amiable hand,
And may the dark pass peacefully by
    As in the hour-glass droops the sand.

Prepare my cornered manchet sweet,
    And in my little crystal cup
Pour out the blithe and flowering mead
    That forthwith I may sup.

Withdraw my curtains from the night,
    And let the crispèd crescent shine
Upon my eyelids while I sleep,
    And soothe me with her beams benign.

From far-away there streams the singing
  Of the mellifluent nightingale,—
Surely if goblins hear her lay,
  They shall not o'er my peace prevail.

Now quench my silver lamp, prythee,
  And bid the harpers harp that tune
Fairies which haunt the meadowlands
  Sing clearly to the stars of June.

And bid them play, though I in dreams
  No longer heed their pining strains,
For I would not to silence wake
  When slumber o'er my senses wanes.

You Angels bright who me defend,
  Enshadow me with curvèd wing,
And keep me in the darksome night
  Till dawn another day do bring.

THE CHILD IN THE STORY AWAKES

The light of dawn rose on my dreams,
  And from afar I seemed to hear
In sleep the mellow blackbird call
  Hollow and sweet and clear.

I prythee, Nurse, my casement open,
  Wildly the garden peals with singing,
And hooting through the dewy pines
  The goblins all are winging.

O listen the droning of the bees,
  That in the roses take delight!
And see a cloud stays in the blue
  Like an angel still and bright.

The gentle sky is spread like silk,
  And, Nurse, the moon doth languish there,
As if it were a perfect jewel
  In the morning's soft-spun hair.

THE CHILD IN THE STORY AWAKES

The greyness of the distant hills
   Is silvered in the lucid East,
See, now the sheeny-plumèd cock
   Wags haughtily his crest.

'O come you out, O come you out,
   Lily, and lavender, and lime;
The kingcup swings his golden bell,
   And plumpy cherries drum the time.

'O come you out, O come you out!
   Roses, and dew, and mignonette,
The sun is in the steep blue sky,
   Sweetly the morning star is set.'

THE LAMPLIGHTER

When the light of day declineth,
And a swift angel through the sky
Kindleth God's tapers clear,
With ashen staff the lamplighter
Passeth along the darkling streets
To light our earthly lamps;

Lest, prowling in the darkness,
The thief should haunt with quiet tread,
Or men on evil errands set;
Or wayfarers be benighted;
Or neighbours bent from house to house
Should need a guiding torch.

He is like a needlewoman
Who deftly on a sable hem
Stitches in gleaming jewels;
Or, haply, he is like a hero,
Whose bright deeds on the long journey
Are beacons on our way.

And when in the East cometh morning,
And the broad splendour of the sun,
Then, with the tune of little birds
Ringing on high, the lamplighter
Passeth by each quiet house,
And putteth out the lamps.

CECIL

Ye little elves, who haunt sweet dells,
Where flowers with the dew commune,
I pray you hush the child, Cecil,
    With windlike song.

O little elves, so white she lieth,
Each eyelid gentler than the flow'r
Of the bramble, and her fleecy hair
    Like smoke of gold.

O little elves, her hands and feet
The angels muse upon, and God
Hath shut a glimpse of Paradise
    In each blue eye.

O little elves, her tiny body
Like a white flake of snow it is,
Drooping upon the pale green hood
    Of the chill snowdrop.

O little elves, with elderflower,
And pimpernel, and the white hawthorn,
Sprinkle the journey of her dreams:
    And, little elves,

Call to her magically sweet,
Lest of her very tenderness
She do forsake this rough brown earth
    And return to us no more.

I MET AT EVE

I met at eve the Prince of Sleep,
His was a still and lovely face,
He wandered through a valley steep
   Lovely in a lonely place.

His garb was grey of lavender,
About his brows a poppy-wreath
Burned like dim coals, and everywhere
   The air was sweeter for his breath.

His twilight feet no sandals wore,
His eyes shone faint in their own flame,
Fair moths that gloomed his steps before
   Seemed letters of his lovely name.

His house is in the mountain ways,
A phantom house of misty walls,
Whose golden flocks at evening graze,
   And witch the moon with muffled calls.

I MET AT EVE

Upwelling from his shadowy springs
Sweet waters shake a trembling sound,
There flit the hoot-owl's silent wings,
   There hath his web the silkworm wound.

Dark in his pools clear visions lurk,
And rosy, as with morning buds,
Along his dales of broom and birk
   Dreams haunt his solitary woods.

I met at eve the Prince of Sleep,
His was a still and lovely face,
He wandered through a valley steep,
   Lovely in a lonely place.

LULLABY

Sleep, sleep, lovely white soul!
The singing mouse sings plaintively,
The sweet night-bird in the chesnut-tree—
They sing together, bird and mouse,
In starlight, in darkness, lonely, sweet,
The wild notes and the faint notes meet—
   Sleep, sleep, lovely white soul!

Sleep, sleep, lovely white soul!
Amid the lilies floats the moth,
The mole along his galleries goeth
In the dark earth; the summer moon
Looks like a shepherd through the pane
Seeking his feeble lamb again—
   Sleep, sleep, lovely white soul!

Sleep, sleep, lovely white soul!
Time comes to keep night-watch with thee
Nodding with roses; and the sea

Saith 'Peace! Peace!' amid his foam
White as thy night-clothes; 'O be still!'
The wind cries up the whisp'ring hill—
  Sleep, sleep, lovely white soul!

ENVOY

THERE clung three roses to a stem,
Did all their hues of summer don,
But came a wind and troubled them,
   And all were gone.

I heard three bells in unison
Clap out some transient heart's delight,
Time and the hour brought silence on
   And the dark night.

Doth not Orion even set !
O love, love, prove true alone,
Till youthful hearts ev'n love forget,
   Then, child, begone !